Tales

from the
Leaking Boot

Matt Black

First published 2018 by IRON Press
5 Marden Terrace
Cullercoats
North Shields
NE30 4PD
tel +44(0)191 2531901
ironpress@xlnmail.com
www.ironpress.co.uk

ISBN 978-0-9954579-2-8
Printed by imprintdigital.com

Cover artwork by Jackie Prachek
Cover and book design Brian Grogan and Peter Mortimer

Typeset in Georgia
IRON Press books are distributed by NBN International
and represented by Inpress Ltd
Churchill House, 12 Mosley Street,
Newcastle upon Tyne, NE1 1DE
tel: +44(0)191 2308104
www.inpressbooks.co.uk

Supported using public funding by
ARTS COUNCIL
ENGLAND

Matt Black lives in Leamington Spa. He was Derbyshire Poet Laureate (2011-2013) and his most recent collection for adults is *Spoon Rebellion* (Smith Doorstop, 2017), and for children *The Owl and the Pussycat and the Turtles of Fun* (Two Rivers Press, 2014).

His poems are published in magazines such as *Staple, The Rialto, The North* and *Magma*, and he has won awards and commissions. He has performed at festivals in the U.K. and toured in Europe and America. He invented the world's first Poetry Jukebox which he uses regularly at festivals and schools. His first play, *The Storm Officer*, is touring in 2018-2019.

www.matt-black.co.uk

THE BIRTH OF THE LEAKING BOOT

LUCKY ACCIDENTS - THAT PROCESS BY WHICH SOMETHING happens by chance and magic is found - are fundamental to my writing process, and to my life. This collection has arisen from a series of lucky accidents. By accident, through work on street poetry at Cheltenham Literature Festival, I met a force of nature, Thom the World Poet, Australian by birth, long time Texan resident. Thom has deep powers of observation and understanding, and an awesome gift for creating instant oral poems, at poetry events, that weave together witty hymns of love and perception about people in the room, or the whole group, or the iniquities of the state machine.

Thom also tirelessly runs Open Mic nights in Texas, and he kindly invited me to tour Austin, Houston and San Antonio. Inspired by his instant response poems, but without his gift for creating them on the spot, on the first day of the tour I decided it would be an interesting experiment, as my version of instant response poems, to write a few haiku that day which I could feed back to our audience in the evening, reflecting my first-time experience of the strange, contradictory world that is Texas, USA.

The first night audience enjoyed them, so I carried on. Haiku quickly seemed a gift for this purpose because they were short, so I could redraft them fast, and work them up quickly, over a coffee in Dairy Queen, or on a Greyhound bus. As instant impressionistic records of what I was seeing they married perfectly into the haiku principle of the physical and the immediate, whilst I also soon discovered that the principle of a meditative or reflective purpose within a haiku could be delightfully (in my view) subverted as part of the transient travel process. "We're going too fast to make these more reflective" is, I think, part of what I am trying to achieve. And other subversive elements sneaked in quickly - ordinary, colloquial and slang dialogue and how that affects haiku, and the potential for the third line to occasionally be more like a joke's punch-line than the change of angle in the third line that haiku conventionally ask us to work at in order to unlock meaning.

Having enjoyed them in Texas, I became addicted to them as a pastime on travels, and an interesting diary record, firstly on tour in Germany, and then 5 years later on holiday in Turkey. In the back of my mind I felt a collection was growing, and another lucky accident, taking a group of wild sixth formers on a writing day to Cleethorpes, led to the final set which seemed to bring them all home in an interesting way. The final happy accident was the statue of the leaking boot, and discovering how that weaves Texas and Germany back into the Cleethorpes narrative. So a title was born, and once you've hit a title, you can't really look back. My very big thanks go to Peter Mortimer, and Iron Press, for bringing these together in a beautiful book, and for joyously embracing these slightly scurrilous versions of haiku, and putting them alongside and amongst his fabulous stable.

Matt Black – March 2018

CONTENTS

1
An Innocent
Englishman in Texas

Day 1

Texas wins ball game.
Man-giant leads whole plane singing
*The Eyes of Texas are Upon You**

Shoes checked on entry,
airport x-ray, security -
watch out, it just might get you

Sweet donut breezes,
traffic-light pizza sellers -
watch out, it just might get you

Blue wind, soft light, long
peaceful street, strawberry cake -
watch out, it just might get you

Day 2

First day fun, browsing
Walmart for what I might need -
toothpaste, rifles, fruit

Angel Pest Control -
We'll Control Those Little Devils
without the U.N.

Texas sunset, steak
horizon below glowing neon
barbecue sauces

First night heckler: *We
wooped your aaaass in 1776.
Was that my aass, sir?*

Day 4

Texas Justice TV judge
says: *All you gotta do is*
scratch your mad place

American TV,
the real monster, not the wee
tim'rous British beastie

Giant road-side sign says
Vasectomy Reversals Here -
at sixty miles an hour

British poets meet
USA poets in International
House Of Pancakes

Day 5

*Texas Is Bigger Than France** -
and a horse with three nostrils
expels too much air

Grits, sausage, eggs, toast,
waffles, coffee, extra cream -
don't mess with breakfast

* *Texas is Bigger Than France* and *Don't Mess With Texas* are phrases
regularly seen in Texas on car stickers, posters etc.

16

Right to work, bail bonds,
no welfare, no state housing -
Don't Mess With Texas

High noon in 6th Street.
First to draw, English cowboy -
Oh, frightfully sorry

Day 6

Imagine the Queen
on Texas Justice TV - *Ma'am, yo sure
bin whippin' their asses*

*My husband and I
ain't listening to that shit,
yo motherfucker*

Dairy Queen, Burger King,
Minute Maid, Jack In The Box -
your royal family

Day 7

Highway exit 191 -
*Gently Resisting Change Since
1872*

Day 8

Stars and stripes everywhere,
porches, stores, gardens, malls -
God Bless America

Fast food, freedom dreams,
police in schools, prom queens -
God Bless America

Rednecks, disabled,
blacks, poor: riding the Greyhounds -
the road not taken

Day 9

Plane nerves: terrorists -
Delta on-flight shows Star Wars,
The Empire Strikes Back

English tourist offers
imperialist guilt evening classes
before it's too late

2
Frühstück is
more than just
a time of day

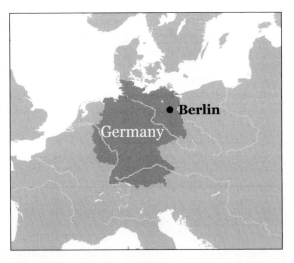

Day 1

Icarus, Heathrow.
Nervous. Shop sells flight cool look -
camera, newspaper, shades

Big screens, CNN,
loud news. Have I just landed
in Texas, Europe?

Day 2

Damp house, no milk, cold.
Dark books haunt wooden table -
Puritan freedom

Gothic letters, Angst,
serious art, padded jackets -
watch out, it just might get you

Luther, Heidegger,
weltschmerz with apfelstrüdel -
watch out, it just might get you

Day 3

First workshop. Finding
international words for love -
haar, kiss, pokochac

*Your first language is
like glue inside you*: a new
language, a new you

Working day: wake, cheese,
windfarm in headlights, school, cheese,
evening, laughter, cheese

Day 4

Swan-necked bicycles,
long straight roads, big horizons -
Slow Progress is Best

Bicycles slip over
old borders, moving quietly
like tectonic plates

Day 5

Hiding in English
shy young minds start burning
new language candles

They discuss - open -
breakfast, Jews, world conflicts. We
don't mention the war

Them to us: is this
really your life? Fish and chips,
the Queen, Mister Bean

Us: we also lie,
drink too much, say sorry, have
high suicide rates

Them: you also queue,
polite, talk weather, have more
teenage pregnancy

Day 7

East, to grand housing,
wide, clean streets. Leninstraβe -
cobbled Utopia

Soft light, KarlMarxstraβe.
Food sufficient in theory
but there's no pudding

Firm Soviet mattress.
Small, early breakfast. The young
just dream of leaving

Day 8

River Oder, serious,
strong current between two countries,
silver fish sliding

River Oder, serious,
border, passports, scrutiny -
cold eyes, fish control

Large, middle-aged couple
eat sausage, sit patiently
in horse-themed café

Day 9

This landmass stretches
to Moscow, Mumbai, Beijing -
our tiny island

Borders, geese, migration.
Big sky says - whose language here?
Morning syntax of light

Nazi graffiti.
Russian roofs, McDonalds, cake -
watch out, it just might get you

Day 10

Schumacher frühstuck -
muesli, rolls, cheese, lap record
for fresh pineapple

Icarus wishes
that if he falls, he falls
amongst friendly fishes

Manchester station:
drunks, no coffee, cheap pasty.
Drizzle. Welcome Home

3
Revert to
Lizard

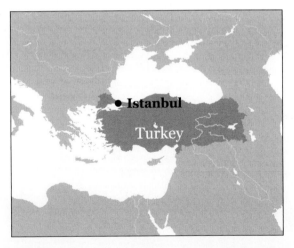

Day 1

Arrival: Asia.
Ten pounds for visa, merhabar*
heat, pine smell, camel

Mountains, orange groves.
Bumpy, ancient continent -
shanty towns glowing

* merhabar: hello

Mama's warm welcome,
dolmades, melon, midnight swim.
Grasshopper soundtrack

Day 2

Small fishing port wakes.
Old boat cafés serve ayran,*
gentleness, tea, time

Clear mermaid river
swirls to sea. Silt spells "Drink me"
in Turkish coffee

---

* Ayran: salty yoghourt drink, favourite of locals;
delicious – if you like it!

Afternoon shimmer.
Fig trees, lemons, olives - doze,
revert to lizard

Day 3

Motorbike panniers made
of Turkish carpet fly by
on Sultan 50

Pahlamin, çay, chill
in zen café, moons of dough -
other world manna

Kiymali gözleme,
fresh chillis, mince, sweet onions,
heaven in a wrap

Posse of Mamas
in town. Slow, powerful, flowing
river of headscarves

Midnight, shops open.
Walking warm streets, inhale
fish, drains, Marlboro

Raki. Eucalyptus
branches rush, wild brushstrokes -
sky sways, drunk again

Day 5

Loose dogs on old rugs,
sprawled huddles, homeless, smiles -
wild pink oleander

Framed Attaturk photos.
Look, our saviour is watching -
intense, winged eyebrows

Day 6

Market music cries -
Baiheer, baiheer, baiheer, baaii,
Baiheer, baiheer, baaii

How much? Twenty? Why?
It depends who you are, plus
your hat, expensive

Hubble bubble pipes,
mystical. Pomegranate
tea, pink, chemical

Day 7

Gentle old men play
fast dominoes amongst wives'
Vodaphone ringtones

Muzzein grief-song wails,
tinny tannoy ululates -
last train, Eternal Bliss

Turkish bath masseur
scrubs, soaps, unveils secret
Roman Emperor

Sad-eyed masseur's huzün,*
country's chaos, wars and loss -
the elephant song

---

* Huzün: melancholy, of a particularly Turkish variety

Day 8

Washday, Aegean breeze,
Helen of Troy hangs out skirts -
siren songs swirling

Boat to Cedir Island.
Byzantine ruins, lizards, sun -
the end of the world

Running and jumping
off long pier into sheer deep green -
the world wakes again

Day 9

Farewells, kind people.
*Teshekur ederim.**
Güle güle

Muzzein grief-song wails,
tinny tannoy ululates -
next plane, English drizzle

* Teshekur ederim: Thank you
   Güle güle: the goodbye being said
   by the person being departed from

57

4
Tales from the Leaking Boot

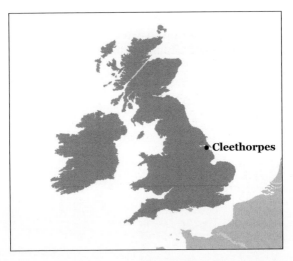

Cleethorpes

Doncaster, Grimsby,
flat fields, fish factory, *last stop
Cleethorpes*: the dream starts here

Desert beach stretching.
Proud old donkey led by
Lawrence of Lincolnshire

First café: builders' tea,
Danish bacon buttie with
Viking horizon

English seaside theme:
big Barnaby Bear welcome
to Fantasy World

Elvis, Pots of Gold,
Spinna Winna, Ding Dong Bells,
fruit machine heaven

Tuppence machines, sliding
tides of moon-coins. Big eyes wait
for brass waves to break

Flippa Winna, Ain't
Life Grand, Knickers for a Knicker,
Pouches for a Pound

On the fun coast, smell
donuts, fish, beer. Hunt bargains
in damp second-hand shop

Brown Humber edgeland
welcomes all sorts. Unique Mecca
where vegans gather

Small statue in pond.
Boy holds up leaking boot. Water,
stories, drip from toe

Boy Immigrant - bronze
mold from Texas, transported
from Germany

Low tide, maze water.
Sand jellies with goosepimples.
Cold, blancmange sky, shakes

Litter of wet shells -
starfish, butterfly mussels,
razors, giant's toenail

Chips, ice-cream, chips.
Saucy postcard - Mine's A Large One.
Look - willies! bums! tits!

Seagulls busy-eyed
as grannies. The town motto -
Vigilantes

Watchful. Like local
fishermen who oversee
deep, swirling cod-world

Bucket and Spade pub.
Drunk holiday eyes watch ferries
bound for Amsterdam

Cleethorpes charm, winking
sun, despite cheap flights - Texas,
Germany, Turkey

Bed and breakfasts, blue sky,
railings where kids skip along -
the dream lives on

Jonny Donut watches
ice-cream sunsets, dirty clouds,
looking for angels

IRON Press is among the country's longest
established independent literary publishers.
The press began operations in 1973 with IRON
Magazine which ran for 83 editions until 1997.
Since 1975 we have also brought out a regular list of
individual collections of poetry, fiction and drama
plus various anthologies ranging from *The Poetry of
Perestroika*, through *Limerick Nation,
100 Island Poems* and *Cold Iron, Ghost Stories
from the 21st Century.*

The press is one of the leading independent
publishers of haiku in the UK.
Since 2013 we have also run a regular IRON Press
Festival round the harbour in our native Cullercoats.
IRON in the Soul, our third festival,
took place in Summer 2017 a fourth festival
is planned for 2019.

We are delighted to be a part of
Inpress Ltd, which was set up by Arts Council
England to support independent literary publishers.
Go to our website (www.ironpress.co.uk)
for full details of our titles and activities.